Speech Bubbles 1

Speech Bubbles 1 is the first set in an exciting new series of picture books designed to be used by Speech Language Therapists/Pathologists, parents/caregivers, and teachers with children who have delayed or disordered speech sound development, children receiving speech therapy, or by those wanting to provide sound awareness activities for their children.

The set includes eleven picture books that each target a different speech sound within the story. The set is also accompanied by a user guide with notes for professionals and caregivers alike. Eleven different speech sounds have been chosen that are early developing sounds, or sounds commonly targeted in speech language therapy: /t/, /d/, /m/, /n/, /p/, /b/, /k/, /g/, /f/, /s/ and /s/ blends. With titles such as *Who Bit My Tail?*, *Crocodiles Can't Climb Trees* and *Ben the Bubble Bear*, the stories are light and engaging, with colourful and fun pictures on every page to keep the child interested.

Perfect not just for therapy, but also for encouraging early sound awareness and development, *Speech Bubbles 1* will create the perfect relaxed learning and practice environment for children beginning their journey into phonological awareness, speech sounds and their positions in words.

Melissa Palmer is a Speech Language Therapist. She has worked for the Ministry of Education, Special Education in New Zealand from 2008 to 2013, with children aged primarily between 2 and 8 years of age. She also completed a diploma in children's writing in 2009 studying under author Janice Marriott, through the New Zealand Business Institute. Melissa has a passion for articulation and phonology, as well as writing and art, and has combined these two loves to create *Speech Bubbles*.

Speech Bubbles 1 (Picture Books and Guide)

Supporting Speech Sound Development in Children

Melissa Palmer

Routledge
Taylor & Francis Group

LONDON AND NEW YORK

First edition published 2019
by Routledge
2 Park Square, Milton Park, Abingdon, Oxon, OX14 4RN

and by Routledge
52 Vanderbilt Avenue, New York, NY 10017

Routledge is an imprint of the Taylor & Francis Group, an informa business

British Library Cataloguing-in-Publication Data
A catalogue record for this book is available from the British Library

Library of Congress Cataloging-in-Publication Data
A catalog record has been requested for this book

ISBN: 978-0-367-18552-7 (set)
ISBN: 978-1-138-54444-4 (pbk)

Typeset in Calibri
by Apex CoVantage, LLC
Printed and bound by CPI Group (UK) Ltd, Croydon, CR0 4YY

For James

What's in the pack?

User Guide

Don't Feed the Dog!

Who Bit My Tail?

Ben the Bubble Bear

Polly's Pink Paint

Gus the Gulping Goat

Crocodiles Can't Climb Trees

Where's Mummy Mouse?

A Bunny Called Noodle

Muffin the Fish

Sally's Sandcastles

Steven the Snail

User Guide contents

User Guide contents

Introduction

This series of picture books is designed to be used with children aged predominantly between 2 and 8 years old. This age range is when children typically develop a wide range of speech sounds used in their speech.

In this pack, you will find eleven picture books and this user guide. The sounds targeted are: /t/, /d/, /p/, /b/, /g/, /k/, /f/, /n/, /m/, /s/, and /s/ blends. This range includes early developing sounds, as well as sounds that are frequently targeted in speech therapy during the early years. Other sounds will be covered in future packs.

These books can be used by Speech Language Therapists/Pathologists, teachers and parents/caregivers. The stories are designed to be read aloud to the child by an adult. This enables the adult to draw attention to the target sound, and to provide a correct model for the child to hear multiple times and in different positions within a word. This includes the sound by itself (in isolation), the beginning of words (in initial position), in middle position (medial position) and at the end of words (final position). It also provides a model of what these words then sound like within sentences. Children love to read stories again and again, and this process of repetition gives the child lots of exposure to the target sound.

Each story targets a specific speech sound. The target sound has been underlined and made in bold to bring attention to it within each story, so the reader is guided to where to place emphasis while reading. Please note that while letters are underlined in the stories, it is not the letters that are the target, it is the sound they make. Blends (which are two consonant sounds without a vowel in between) with the target sound in them are not underlined, as these are much more difficult to pronounce. The only exception is 'Steven the Snail' which targets /s/ blends. Please refer to the notes on each individual story for more information.

These books are not designed to replace receiving speech language therapy when necessary; they were developed to be used alongside speech therapy. They can also be used as a fun and engaging activity to promote speech sound development for children within the home as well as at schools, kindergartens and centres.

If you have concerns about your child's speech sound development, please refer to a Speech Language Therapist/Pathologist for an assessment.

USeS

For Speech Language Therapists/ Pathologists

These picture books are designed to be used as an activity during the therapy session, or as 'homework' with families of a child receiving therapy.

They are designed to be used as an auditory bombardment type activity, especially for those children who are reluctant to participate in therapy. This way, it is a non-confrontational activity where the child first listens, but is not expected to use the target sound themselves or repeat words etc. If the child is comfortable repeating sounds and words, then the books could also be used for this as well.

The chosen sound is targeted in isolation, medial and final position and also in isolation so it can be used as an activity no matter at what stage of therapy the child is currently.

The target sound is underlined and in bold to draw attention to it, but is a guideline only. These words could potentially be used as target words, which you could get your client to repeat after you, or once they are more familiar with the story, you could pause while reading and they say the word themselves. In this way, you can use the story throughout the stages of therapy – e.g. if targeting the sound in isolation, encourage the client to make the target sound at the appropriate moment of the story. If you are targeting a sound in initial position, focus on those words in the story and ask the child to say the word. This can work when targeting two word phrases and then longer sentences.

The sounds underlined are those that are in more simple words e.g. no blends, or next to another consonant sound. However, in the majority of the books, these more difficult words are still included and could also be targeted should you choose. Both single syllable and two to three syllable words have also been included in the underlining, so there is also the possibility of further simplifying your targets if required.

For parents/caregivers and teachers

This series of picture books is designed predominantly as a listening activity for the children. The purpose is for the adult to read the story with the chosen target sound to the child, giving the child many different and correct examples of how to use the sound, and the sound within words and sentences. If being used as a listening activity, the child would not be expected to participate in the story e.g. repeating words or sounds after you, but rather would listen to how you use the sound within the words and story. The repetition of the target sound within words increases the frequency to which the child hears the sound. The more the child hears it, the more likely they will hear the difference between what they are currently using and the correct pronunciation of the sound/word. This makes this picture book series also very useful for those children who are shy, and those who may be aware that people find them hard to understand and are reluctant to participate themselves.

If the child is willing to participate, you may like to ask them to repeat a word or sound after you, or if the child is familiar with the story, pause to see if they will fill in the gap. If the child uses the sound correctly, be sure to praise them with positive reinforcement e.g. "Good talking, that was a great /s/ sound". If they don't use it correctly, do not say anything negative e.g. "that was wrong, you say it like this". Negative feedback may cause the child to not participate at all, and the aim of the picture books is to create a fun, positive and relaxed learning environment. Focus on the positive, and ignore the negative.

As you look through the books, you will notice that letters have been underlined and made in bold throughout the story. It's important to remember that this is to draw your attention to the <u>sound</u> these letters make, not the actual letters themselves. For example, in the story that targets the /k/ sound, you will see that both the letters 'c' and 'k' have been underlined. This is because in these circumstances, both those letters make a /k/ sound within that word. You may notice as you go through the story, that there will be occasions that letters are not underlined where you may initially think they should be. This may be because the letters are not pronounced as the target sound e.g. in the story targeting the /t/ sound, the letter 't' would not be underlined in the word 'both' as the letters 't' and 'h' combined in this case make a /th/ sound, which is not the target.

Another thing to note is where the target sound is within a blend – which is where two consonant sounds are made together within a word without a vowel in between e.g. /sp/ in 'spoon' – the sound has not been underlined. This is because blends are much harder to use than a single consonant sound by itself. For this reason, there will be other stories targeting common blends in English as a separate target e.g. the story within this pack targeting /s/ blends. Please see the individual pages with notes for each separate book for more details.

If using these picture books without the guidance of a Speech Language Therapist/Pathologist (SLT/P), the recommendation would be to use these picture books as a listening and sound awareness activity. You may like to ask a child to repeat a sound or word after you, but do not place any pressure on the child to do so. If the child has difficulty producing certain speech sounds, and doesn't appear to be improving, it would be advisable to get an assessment from a SLT/P and use the stories in a way that fits into the child's therapy plan.

Notes for individual picture books

Don't Feed the Dog! - targeting /d/ sound

- While reading the story to the child, you could occasionally point out the /d/ sound e.g. "Danny! Don't feed the dog" ... "oh, dog starts with a /d/ sound".

- You could talk about how you make the sound e.g. "I touch the tip of my tongue to the top of my mouth like this ... /d/".

- You could get the child to watch <u>you</u> make the /d/ sound and use a mirror so they can see if they are doing the same as you.

- If the child repeats the word or sound after you correctly, be sure to praise them e.g. "Well done, that was a great /d/ sound". Be sure to focus on the positive rather than the negative – don't point out their mistakes.

Speech Bubbles 1

Underlined /d/ sound within words

Initial (Beginning)	Medial (Middle)	Final (End)
Danny	Daddy	Hated
Danny's	Sounded	Hid
Daddy	Didn't	Bed
Day	Cheddar	Fed
Didn't	Couldn't	Outside
Dog	Teddy	Sounded
Don't	Feeding	Feed
		Had
		Called
		Said
		Tasted
		Mad

Not underlined

Word (reason underlined)	Reason
Window	Two consonants together (blend)
Thunder	
Under	
And	
Understand	
Find	
Sandwiches	

Word (reason underlined)	Reason
Wa**dd**ling To**ld** Fou**nd** Ma**dl**y	
Stompe**d** Looke**d** Like**d**	Not pronounced as a /d/ sound

Who Bit My Tail? - targeting /t/ Sound

- While reading the story to the child, you could occasionally point out the /t/ sound e.g. "Tiger woke up feeling happy" … "oh, Tiger starts with a /t/ sound".

- You could talk about how <u>you</u> make the sound e.g. "I touch the tip of my tongue to the top of my mouth like this … /t/ … and say it really quietly /t/".

- You could get the child to watch <u>you</u> make the /t/ sound, and use a mirror so they can see if they are doing the same as you.

- If the child repeats the word or sound after you correctly, be sure to praise them e.g. "Well done, that was a great /t/ sound". Be sure to focus on the positive rather than the negative – don't point out their mistakes.

Speech Bubbles 1

Underlined /t/ sound within words

Initial (Beginning)	Medial (Middle)	Final (End)
Tiger	Biter	About
Tiger's	Biting	Rat
Teeth	Bitten	At
Tail	Tortoise	What
Tip	Kitten	Great
Tortoise	Fitted	Out
To		Bite
Too		Bit
Tiny		Bat
		Goat
		Put
		Bright
		It

Not underlined

Word (reason underlined)	Reason
Fa**st** Ra**t's** We**nt** Did**n't** Do**n't** Was**n't**	Two consonants together without a vowel in between (blend)
Tee**th** **Th**is **Th**ere **Th**e Mou**th** **Th**en	Doesn't make a /t/ sound – 't' and 'h' make a /th/ sound
Stret**ched** Perfe**ctl**y	More than two consonants together without a vowel in between (cluster)

Ben the Bubble Bear - targeting /b/ sound

- While reading the story to the child, you could occasionally point out the /b/ sound e.g. "Ben the bear loved to blow bubbles" ... "oh, Ben starts with a /b/ sound".

- You could talk about how <u>you</u> make the sound e.g. "I bump my lips together like this ... /b/".

- You could get the child to watch you make the /b/ sound, and use a mirror so they can see if they are doing the same as you.

- If the child repeats the word or sound after you correctly, be sure to praise them e.g. "Well done, that was a great /b/ sound". Be sure to focus on the positive rather than the negative – don't point out their mistakes.

Speech Bubbles 1

Underlined /b/ sound within words

Initial (Beginning)	Medial (Middle)	Final (End)
Ben Ben's Bear Bear's Bubble Bubbles Big Bang Back Biggest	Bubbles	Caleb

Not underlined

Word (reason underlined)	Reason
Blow **Bl**ew **Bl**ue	Two consonants together without a vowel in between (blend)

Polly's Pink Paint - targeting /p/ sound

- While reading the story to the child, you could occasionally point out the /p/ sound e.g. "Polly poured the paint into her mud patch" ... "oh, paint starts with a /p/ sound".

- You could talk about how <u>you</u> make the sound e.g. "I bump my lips together and make a quiet popping noise like this ... /p/".

- You could get the child to watch you make the /p/ sound, and use a mirror so they can see if they are doing the same as you.

- If the child repeats the word or sound after you correctly, be sure to praise them e.g. "Well done, that was a great /p/ sound". Be sure to focus on the positive rather than the negative – don't point out their mistakes.

Underlined /p/ sound within words

Initial (Beginning)	Medial (Middle)	Final (End)
Polly	Apples	Tulip
Polly's	Paper	Up
Pig	Hopping	Hop
Pink	Pepper	
Paint	Happily	
Painted	Happy	
Paintbrush		
Pears		
Paper		
Pickle		
Picked		
Path		
Picket		
Penny		
Parrot		

Initial (Beginning)	Medial (Middle)	Final (End)
Pepper Pussycat Pitter Patter Poured Patch		

Not underlined

Word (reason underlined)	Reason
U**ps**et Dro**pped** Raindro**ps** Di**pped**	Two consonant sounds together without a vowel in between (blend)

Gus the Gulping Goat - targeting /g/ Sound

- While reading the story to the child, you could occasionally point out the /g/ sound e.g. "Along galloped Maggie the goat" … "oh, galloped starts with a /g/ sound".

- You could talk about how <u>you</u> make the sound e.g. "I touch my tongue up to the top of my mouth, at the back and make a gulping sound … /g/".

- You could get the child to watch you make the /g/ sound, making sure the tongue is down at the front, and use a mirror so they can see if they are doing the same as you.

- If the child repeats the word or sound after you correctly, be sure to praise them e.g. "Well done, that was a great /g/ sound". Be sure to focus on the positive rather than the negative – don't point out their mistakes.

Underlined /g/ sound within words

Initial (Beginning)	Medial (Middle)	Final (End)
Gus	Yoghurt	Drag
Goat	Wagon	Jug
Gulp	Maggie	Pig
Gulping	Together	Doug
Gulped	Teegan	Big
Get	Tiger	
Gets	Giggle	
Gallons		
Galloped		
Garden		
Garage		
Got		
Gathered		
Giggling		
Giggle		

Not underlined

Word (reason underlined)	Reason
Gara**ge** Alon**g** Mornin**g** Gulpin**g** Gigglin**g** Gulpin**g**	Not pronounced as a /g/ sound, but as a /dg/ sound
Gi**ggl**ing Pi**gp**en **Gr**abbed **Gl**ee	Two consonants together without a vowel in between (blend)

Crocodiles Can't Climb Trees - targeting /k/ Sound

- While reading the story to the child, you could occasionally point out the /k/ sound e.g. "Once there was a cute monkey called Luca" ... "oh, cute starts with a /k/ sound".

- You could talk about how <u>you</u> make the sound e.g. "I touch my tongue to the top of my mouth at the back and make a quiet sound like this ... /k/".

- You could get the child to watch you make the /k/ sound, and use a mirror so they can see if they are doing the same as you.

- If the child repeats the word or sound after you correctly, be sure to praise them e.g. "Well done, that was a great /k/ sound". Be sure to focus on the positive rather than the negative – don't point out their mistakes.

- You will notice that some 'c' letters have been underlined in the story – this is because sometimes a 'c' can mean a /k/ sound. Remember – it's the <u>sound</u> not the letter itself that is the target.

Speech Bubbles 1

Underlined /k/ sound within words

Initial (Beginning)	Medial (Middle)	Final (End)
Cute	Soccer	Snuck
Kick	Luca	Kick
Kicking	Crocodile	Sack
Kevin	Crocodiles	Rock
Kevin's	Kicking	Thick
Could	Bucket	
Catch	Pickles	
Coming	Thickest	
Capered	Because	
Carrots		
Cut		
Cart		
Corn		
Can't		

Not underlined

Word (reason underlined)	Reason
Mo**nk**ey Ba**nk** **Cr**ocodile **Qu**i**ckl**y Ki**cked** **Cr**ou**ched** Thi**nk** **Cl**imbed Tru**nk** Tu**cked** **Cl**imb Li**ked**	Two consonant sounds together without a vowel in between (blend)

Where's Mummy Mouse? - targeting /m/ Sound

- While reading the story to the child, you could occasionally point out the /m/ sound e.g. "I haven't seen your mummy said Mrs Moose" … "oh, moose starts with a /m/ sound".

- You could talk about how <u>you</u> make the sound e.g. "I put my lips together like this … /m/".

- You could get the child to watch you make the /m/ sound, and use a mirror so they can see if they are doing the same as you.

- If the child repeats the word or sound after you correctly, be sure to praise them e.g. "Well done, that was a great /m/ sound". Be sure to focus on the positive rather than the negative – don't point out their mistakes.

Underlined /m/ sound within words

Initial (Beginning)	Medial (Middle)	Final (End)
Mouse	Mummy	Kim
Mummy	Camel	Warm
Moss	Kimmy	Home
My	Yummy	Time
Moaned		Came
Mat		
Munching		
Mrs		
Mr		
Miss		
Moose		
Mailbox		
Meerkat		
Making		
Music		
Monkey		
Mound		
Mud		
Moon		

Not underlined

Word (reason underlined)	Reason
So**meth**ing	Two consonant sounds together without a vowel in between (blend)

A Bunny Called Noodle - targeting /n/ Sound

- While reading the story to the child, you could occasionally point out the /n/ sound e.g. "Once there was a bunny named Noodle" ... "oh, Noodle starts with a /n/ sound".

- You could talk about how <u>you</u> make the sound e.g. "I touch the tip of my tongue to the top of my mouth behind my teeth like this ... /n/".

- You could get the child to watch you make the /n/ sound, and use a mirror so they can see if they are doing the same as you.

- If the child repeats the word or sound after you correctly, be sure to praise them e.g. "Well done, that was a great /n/ sound". Be sure to focus on the positive rather than the negative – don't point out their mistakes.

Underlined /n/ sound within words

Initial (Beginning)	Medial (Middle)	Final (end)
Noodle	Bunny	Brown
Noodles	Bunnies	An
Name	Downy	Run
Named	Tiny	Green
Nice	Running	Cotton
Nose	Funny	Barn
Noses	Nanny	When
Not	Any	Sun
Night		Down
None		Moon
No		Soon
Need		In
Nervous		None
Never		Can
Nestled		Alone
Next		
Nanny		

Not underlined

Word (reason underlined)	Reason
Inside Bou**nc**ing Bou**nc**e Ru**ns** La**nds** U**n**dersta**nd** I**nd**eed Se**nt** I**gn**ored Lo**ng**er Fi**nd** Frie**nd** Frie**nds** Sou**nd**ed Do**n't** Da**nc**ed Moo**nl**ight E**nd** O**nc**e U**nt**il	Two consonant sounds together without a vowel in between (blend)

Muffin the Fish - targeting /f/ Sound

- While reading the story to the child, you could occasionally point out the /f/ sound e.g. "Muffin the fish was very wide" … "oh, fish starts with a /f/ sound".

- You could talk about how <u>you</u> make the sound e.g. "I touch my teeth to my lips like this and blow like this … /f/".

- You could get the child to watch you make the /f/ sound, and use a mirror so they can see if they are doing the same as you.

- If the child repeats the word or sound after you correctly, be sure to praise them e.g. "Well done, that was a great /f/ sound". Be sure to focus on the positive rather than the negative – don't point out their mistakes.

- You will notice that the letters 'gh' have been underlined in the word 'laugh' – this is because this letter combination makes a /f/ sound. Remember – it's the <u>sound</u> not the letter that is the target.

Underlined /f/ sound within words

Initial (Beginning)	Medial (Middle)	Final (End)
Fish	Muffin	If
Four		Laugh
Funny		Of
Fingers		
Fins		
Fork		
Faces		
Find		
Finding		
Food		
Fact		
Feels		
Feeds		

Not underlined

Word (reason underlined)	Reason
Flaps **Fl**its **Fl**itter **Fl**utter Butter**fl**y's	Two consonant sounds together without a vowel in between (blend)

Sally's Sandcastles - targeting /s/ sound

- While reading the story to the child, you could occasionally point out the /s/ sound e.g. "Sally and her mum were bored" ... "oh, Sally starts with a /s/ sound".

- You could talk about how <u>you</u> make the sound e.g. "I bring my tongue to the front of my mouth behind my teeth, stretch my mouth a little like a smile and blow like this ... /s/".

- You could get the child to watch you make the /s/ sound, and use a mirror so they can see if they are doing the same as you.

- If the child repeats the word or sound after you correctly, be sure to praise them e.g. "Well done, that was a great /s/ sound". Be sure to focus on the positive rather than the negative – don't point out their mistakes.

- You will notice some 'c' letters underlined as well as 's'. This is because for the word, the letter 'c' indicated a /s/ sound. Remember – it's about the <u>sound</u> not the letters.

Underlined /s/ sound within words

Initial (Beginning)	Medial (Middle)	Final (End)
Sally	Sandcastles	House
Sitting	Sandcastle	Houses
See	Decided	Sandcastles
Sun	Visit	Was
Sunny	Disappeared	Seashells
So	Houses	Sandwiches
Said		Yes
Sand		Use
Suddenly		
Saw		
Some		
Sandcastles		
Sandcastle		
Sea		
Sat		
Soon		
Surrounded		

Initial (Beginning)	Medial (Middle)	Final (End)
City Seashells Sandwiches Sadly Sorry		

Not underlined

Word (reason underlined)	Reason
Ou**ts**ide E**xc**itedly I**t's** **Sp**ade I**ts**elf Sandcast**les** Fir**st** Ju**st** **Sw**im	Two consonant sounds together without a vowel in between (blend) (Asked has three consonant sounds together – called a cluster)

Speech Bubbles 1

Word (reason underlined)	Reason
Swimming **Spl**at **Sl**id Seashe**lls** A**sked** **Sw**oosh Mu**st** **Sm**iled That**'s** Le**t's**	

Steven the Snail - targeting /s/ blends

- While reading the story to the child, you could occasionally point out the /s/ sound in words with blends e.g. "slid under a brown stool" ... "oh, stool starts with a /s/ sound".

- You could talk about how <u>you</u> make the sound e.g. "I bring my tongue to the front of my mouth behind my teeth, stretch my mouth a little like a smile and blow like this ... /s/".

- You could get the child to watch you make the /s/ sound, and use a mirror so they can see if they are doing the same as you.

- If the child repeats the word or sound after you correctly, be sure to praise them e.g. "Well done, that was a great /s/ sound". Be sure to focus on the positive rather than the negative – don't point out their mistakes.

- Often children will drop the /s/ sound in words that start with an /s/ blend. This story is to bring attention to the /s/ at the beginning.

Underlined /s/ blends within words – all in initial position

St	Sp	Sl	Sn	Sm	Sw
Steven	Special	Slowly	Snail	Small	Swam
Steven's	Spotty	Slid	Snow		
Stone	Spikey	Sleeping	Sneaked		
Stool	Spoon		Snake		
	Spider				

Not underlined

Word (reason underlined)	Reason
Stream **Spr**ing	Three consonant sounds together without vowels in between – called a cluster. Could still be a target, however they are more difficult to use than blends due to the extra sound